STRAIGHTEN THE PATH

A Unique Approach for Job Seekers

JOHN FREEZE

STRAIGHTEN THE PATH

A Unique Approach for Job Seekers

John Freeze

All Rights Reserved

Copyright © 2014 John Freeze

Scripture taken from the THE HOLY BIBLE, NEW INTERNATIONAL VERSION®, Copyright © 1973, 1978, 1984 by International Bible Society. Used by permission of Zondervan. All rights reserved.

No part of this publication may be reproduced, distributed, or transmitted in any form or by any means, including photocopying, recording, or other electronic or mechanical methods, without the prior written permission of the author, except in the case of brief quotations embodied in critical reviews and certain other noncommercial uses permitted by copyright laws of the United States of America.

ISBN-13: 978-1505450545

Edited by Diane Simmons Dill, *Right*Write Productions, LLC
www.facebook.com/RightwriteProductions

Cover Design: John Freeze

Interior Design and Formatting by Diane Simmons Dill, *Right*Write Productions, LLC

Cover Artwork by Ryan Richie.
Line Art: Copyright www.123rf.com/profile_pilart, 123RF Stock Photo, Image # 10725169.

Printed in the United States of America

TABLE OF CONTENTS

INTRODUCTION 1
CHAPTER 1: THE DILEMMA 7
CHAPTER 2: "SAYS WHO?!" 15
CHAPTER 3: WHY DO I NEED A JOB? 23
CHAPTER 4: "WHAT DO YOU DO?" 35
CHAPTER 5: YOUR RESUME – TELLING OTHERS ABOUT YOUR SKILLS AND EXPERIENCES 39
CHAPTER 6: WHOM CAN YOU TRUST? 51
CHAPTER 7: EVERYONE NEEDS A SHERPA TO KEEP THEM ON THE PATH 63
CHAPTER 8: NETWORKING – TURNS OUT THE UGLY TRUTH CAN BE A BEAUTIFUL THING! 71
CHAPTER 9: THE PROVEN PATH 83
CHAPTER 10: TALES FROM THE PATH 87
CHAPTER 11: FINAL THOUGHTS 103

Dedication

This book is dedicated to my amazing wife, Sharon, whose courage, grace, and wisdom continue to inspire me. Sometimes we've skipped along the path. Sometimes we have crawled along the path. Sometimes we've been on a full-out sprint, struggling to stay on the path. But we've travelled every inch of the path together. And for that, I am thankful to our God, who brought us together and keeps us together.

I love you, Sharon!

Acknowledgement

This book has been in the works for many years. There are so many people I'd like to thank for encouraging me and for providing me with insights along the way.

Thank you to Bill Pavelich, Matthew Fleming, John Gaillard, Jon O'Nan, and Romie Horton, for coaching and mentoring me, pushing me, and challenging me in my walk along the path. I am forever grateful for your investment into my life.

To Eric Bolin, Paul Stokey, and countless others who have allowed me to walk with them, as they have walked with me, through multiple career changes and job searches throughout the years; your prayers and insights have been priceless.

I would like to thank my editor, Diane Dill. You have no idea what a blessing you have been to me in this process. Had you not reached out to me when I had no idea what to do next, this book would likely still reside on my computer, where no one could see it. I appreciate you and thank God for you, and for your gifts of wisdom and encouragement. You are making a difference!

Finally, I am in awe of the Creator of the universe, who placed this book on my heart and kept it alive until the right time. All glory to Him, who sits on the throne.

Proverbs 3:5-6

Trust in the LORD with all your heart
and lean not on your own understanding;
in all your ways acknowledge him,
and he will make your paths straight.

Luke 3:5

Every valley shall be filled in,
every mountain and hill made low.
The crooked roads shall become straight,
the rough ways smooth.

Introduction

My primary study Bible resembles a filing cabinet almost as much as it does a book. I decided when I got this Bible that I was REALLY going to use this one. All sorts of notes are scribbled in the margins; pictures are crammed in between the pages; and cards, notes, and study outlines are stuffed inside the back cover. Of all this "stuff," there are two things that haunt me. One is a small scrap of paper that my grandfather placed in a Bible he and my grandmother gave to me when I was about 13. Like most 13-year-old boys, I didn't open that Bible much. As a matter of fact, I did not find the small note "Papa Jack" had placed inside until many years after his death. The handwritten note looks like this:

> Note:
> Words of Wisdom To Guide, And direct Your Paths of Life; see "Proverbs 3:1-12", with Spec. Note To, "3:5 and 6".

I'll be honest with you. I regret not finding and reading these verses until I was in my late 20s. Since then, these gems of wisdom from God's Word have become the foundation of my faith.

> *Trust in the Lord with all your heart, and lean not on your own understanding; in all your ways acknowledge him, and he will make your paths straight. (Proverbs 3:5:6)*

As a 13-year-old boy, there is absolutely no reason not to lean on your own understanding. After all, you already know everything! Nearing age fifty, I finally have come to understand how little I do understand. I am also convinced that living out these two simple verses in every facet of life is a major key to success, happiness, and pleasing God.

The second piece of paper that has "haunted" me for about fifteen years is a little larger than the first. It's about the size of a standard index card. It looks like this:

MISSION CARD

I will _Write a book._

so that I can bring _others like me & Myself_

closer to Christ.

This card requires some explanation, too. My wonderful wife, Sharon, was the Youth Minister at our church (ok, she isn't ordained and her title was really "director," but I saw her "minister" in ways that make me comfortable with changing her title). I was fortunate enough to tag along on many of the awesome retreats she planned and led. At one retreat, the focus was on understanding our call in the world and how we could make a difference. She had everyone (youth counselors and the youth) fill out a mission card during a small group exercise.

Looking at the card now (over fifteen years since I wrote it), something strikes me as odd. I saw writing a book not only as a way to bring others closer to Christ, but also as a way to bring me closer to him.

One more thing I forgot to mention. I'm not a writer!!! My formal education is in Electrical Engineering and Business. Don't panic—the book doesn't try to draw analogies between faith and flux capacitors or anything like that.

This book is designed to begin to address an issue that has burdened me for a long time. Too many people are miserable in their work and don't know what to do about it. During more than twenty-five years in the corporate world, I have been continually saddened by the number of people, Christians and non-believers alike, who hate what they do, but yet do nothing to change their situation. I hope the book will accomplish two main things:

1. Provide some insight into God's view of your work and your career.

2. Provide a framework and process for allowing God to be your career counselor and recruiter.

For over twenty years, I have held at least ten different jobs. Some I loved, some I hated after the first three weeks, and some just "paid the bills." What I have realized, however, is that when I have allowed God to direct my job searches, I have learned incredible lessons. His power, perfect timing, and grace have been revealed to me more than in anything else I have experienced in my life, with the exception of the adoptions of my two wonderful kids.

INTRODUCTION 5

So, whether you are planning for your first job out of college or feeling trapped in a boring, dead-end job with nowhere to go, help is here. Perhaps you are looking for a new job due to a layoff or simply struggling with the fact that you spend fifty hours a week at this place called work and you aren't sure you are where you are *supposed to be* right now. Whatever your situation, I hope this book will encourage you.

CHAPTER 1

The Dilemma

I stood on a rock in the middle of the river, yelling at the top of my lungs, "What do you want me to do? What do you want? Just tell me and I'll do it. Just tell me what you want me to do!"

Reading these first few lines likely stirs up visions of someone being held at gunpoint, or perhaps someone is about to be pushed into a roaring river by some ultra-sinister bad guy. The truth is, it's a true story. It's about me. And I was yelling at the ultimate "good guy." God. Why was I yelling at him? Allow me to take you back in time and give you a little background information and properly set the stage for the story.

I graduated fourth in my class in high school. I was voted "most likely to succeed" by my fellow students. I went to a great college, got a degree in Electrical Engineering (because I had learned that they make a lot of money!), married my college sweetheart and got a fantastic job with an impressive company right out of college. Sharon and I had recently adopted an incredible baby boy from Paraguay. I know what you are saying. I can't learn anything from this guy's experience. He couldn't relate to my dilemma. He's got it made.

Well, for a while that seemed to be the case. I received rapid promotions in the big company, and by the time I was thirty, I had gotten my MBA and was one of five project managers working on the integration of two $10 billion companies. The merger put the firm squarely onto the Fortune 100 list.

As you might expect, doing this kind of work at such a young age, I was pretty "confident." OK, I'll admit it. I was one arrogant son of a gun! So much so, that I decided I wouldn't be able to grow my career and earnings fast enough in this big, conservative company. I deserved a lot more. I had an engineering degree from a top university, an MBA, and incredible experience that would surely put my resume at the top of any recruiter's pile.

Here's where the problems started. Did you notice that I said "I decided"? Would you like to venture a guess regarding whom I consulted on this decision? Sharon? Nope. My boss? No. My equally aggressive peers? Perhaps. How about God? He had always been a part of my life. I had given him some of the credit for my success, at least in front of my Christian friends. Heck, I had even started a Bible study with some other guys at work a few years ago.

I'd love to be able to tell you about how crucial God was in my decision to take that big leap. But it would be a lie. I did think about God in the process. I was sure that if God gave me the gifts and tools to get this far, surely he wouldn't want those tools sitting around getting rusty. He would want to bless me more by rewarding me with a big title, a bigger paycheck, and the recognition that I so badly wanted.

I told myself and Sharon, "This is it. I'll never be more marketable than I am right now. I'm young; I have the education and the experience to get that big six-figure job, and we will be on our way. This is 'our' big chance." I worked diligently on my resume and started networking. It wasn't long before I found myself sitting in front of the owner of a small, prestigious search firm in town. We weren't talking about how he might help me find a job. We were talking about how I might be a fit in his firm.

The next several weeks I was living off adrenaline. Multiple interviews followed with the same firm. They conducted an extensive interview with an industrial psychologist to see if my "profile was a fit with the job." We started talking salary and when I would become eligible to be a partner of the firm. Finally, after multiple phone calls and face-to-face interviews, one of the partners in the firm called me to say, "all that is really left is for you and your wife to have dinner with the owner and his wife." I'm in! I've done it. I immediately began thinking of what type of car I needed to buy and how I would furnish my new office.

Still working on the merger in my current job, I began to learn of extensive layoffs that were coming. Layoffs would even be affecting the group where I currently reported. Oh my! This is great! I can significantly increase my pay with this new job AND get a big severance package! What will I do with all the money? I decided not to take a risk. I immediately went to the vice-president of my group and said, "I know there are going to be layoffs in our organization. A lot of people are really worried about that, and I wanted to let you know that I've decided it's time for me to leave." She assured me there would be a place for me, but I went on to explain that I really didn't think I was a fit for the rather conservative culture and that after working on the merger, I didn't think there was anything in that company that I really wanted to do. She seemed rather concerned, but told me that while they were not asking for volunteers officially, she would consider my request.

I immediately went to my manager and told him what I had done. He thought I was nuts! First, he thought I was completely out of line for going directly to a vice-president and being so bold in a company where "we just don't do that." Second, he could not comprehend that I would consider leaving at such an exciting time in the life of that company. What did he know?

The last thing in the world I wanted was to end up like him. Taking direction from someone else and sitting still in the same company for twenty-five years would never work for me. For heaven's sake, I'd already been there for over five years!

I went home that afternoon with a little bit of discomfort over the risk I had taken. But on the way home, my mind drifted to other things. My family and I were leaving that afternoon to go to the mountains for a nice weekend away. I knew that my official job offer was coming soon, and I looked forward to the relaxation of a nice weekend away, to ponder what might lie in store for my wife, my young son, and me.

When I arrived home, my wife was packing a few remaining things into a suitcase on the bed. Shortly after I walked in, the phone rang. It was him! What a weekend this is going to be! A chance to celebrate my new career! Almost twenty years later, his words to me are still crystal clear.

"Hi John. This is Chuck. We've decided not to hire anyone right now."

I can't recall anything else he said. I think I made a feeble attempt to convince him that he should hire me, but I knew it was over.

Now. Let's review my situation. I have a great job, but I just told the vice-president to lay me off. The great job that is going to make me (and my family, of course) rich, just crashed and burned. Put that all together, and you get UNEMPLOYED! Oh yeah, and I'm packing the car to go on vacation. This is no time for a relaxing weekend. I have to find a job!

I don't remember the details of the rest of the packing or the drive to the mountains. But what I do remember is that my mind was racing about a million miles an hour trying to solve this dilemma.

I won't go into details, but it is important for you to know that at that point in my life, I was already a Christian. I had gone to church my whole life (except during college...does anyone really go to church during college?). I had truly begun to understand several years earlier how much God loves me. Sharon and I had grown tremendously in our faith as we leaned completely on God during the adoption of our son, Ian. I read the Bible and prayed daily.

So how was this happening to me? I couldn't understand why God had taken that job from me. He must want me to do something else. Something bigger... More important... That's it! He wanted me to do something really special. So he had led me down this path and put me in the position of having to take a big leap of faith. Right? Only one thing was missing from this otherwise "made for TV drama." I had no idea what God wanted me to do.

That brings us to the yelling in the river incident. We arrived at the small cabin we had rented in the mountains and unpacked. Sharon knew I was completely stressed out, and I told her I needed to go for a walk and be alone for a bit. As I hiked down a nearby path, I began to pray. I honestly don't remember what I prayed, but I remember the desperate, scared feeling and the huge knot in my throat and that I was begging God to rescue me and to tell me what to do.

I came to a place where the path ran along a river. I climbed out onto the rocks and stood in the middle of the river and looked up and began screaming at God. I was literally screaming out loud—thank goodness it was a loud river, or Sharon would have likely called 911! I was angry that God had put me in this predicament if he wasn't going to tell me what to do. I stood in that river yelling, "I'll go to seminary!! I'll be a missionary!! Just tell me what you want!! Tell me!! Tell me, and I'll do anything!!"

God answered with silence.

I knew that I was sincere. At that moment, I would have done whatever God asked of me. But he was silent... When you make yourself completely vulnerable to someone like I was doing with God, silence is not what you are hoping to hear. I swear I was expecting a burning bush, a talking owl, or something extraordinary like that. Instead, I got silence.

I was furious. Why would God toy with me like this? He takes away my job to get my attention. I listen. I plead. But he is silent.

CHAPTER 2

"Says Who?!"

I went back to the cabin where we were staying and plopped down on the bed. Too tired to cry, I just laid there exhausted. As I prayed for God to protect me and my family, it hit me...

God had never said I needed a new job. I never even asked him if he thought it was a good idea. Like a ton of bricks, it hit me. I'm responsible for this predicament, not God! I had put my family in jeopardy in order for me to have a shot at fame and fortune. The truth of the matter was that Sharon hadn't agreed with the move. She saw no need for a change.

> **LESSON: Before you head down the path of finding a new job, make sure God endorses a change.**

Let's take a look at some of the reasons that people decide they "need" a job change. Some of the more common things I hear from folks are:

- *I'm bored.*
- *I know that I'm capable of much more than this.*
- *I'm worth more than this job is paying me.*
- *I'm traveling too much.*
- *I have so much more potential than this.*
- *I'm not appreciated at my current job.*
- *I always wanted to be a _____ (doctor, lawyer, accountant, etc...)*
- *I need more money so I can take better care of my family.*

Notice that each of these common reasons starts with "I." There are obviously lots of other reasons why people change jobs, but I hear these a lot. Are these good reasons? I can't decide that for you. Some of them might be legitimate, but I fear that for many people, the reasons above are actually disguises for motives such as:

- *I'm jealous of the other people I know who are always bragging about their jobs and have a bigger house than I do.*
- *I want more stuff.*
- *I like the idea of telling people I'm a VP!*
- *I need to feel more wanted.*

- *I want people to be impressed when I talk about my job.*
- *I'm not happy with my family life, so I need something to keep life exciting.*
- *I can do anything I set my mind to do. I should never be satisfied; that would be laziness. (As youngsters, we are taught ideas such as this.)*

There are also numerous people who have decided to find another job, yet can't articulate a solid reason at all for feeling that way. Sadly, especially for men, we have been taught by the world that being in a continuous job search makes us seem more confident and important to others. I wish I had a stock option for every time I've heard someone say, "I've always got my eyes open for something better." The problem with such a mindset is that people find very few jobs by simply "keeping your eyes open" (more on that later). More importantly, saying that you are "always looking" portrays that there is something wrong with being content where you are. That's just not biblical. Paul provides a beautiful illustration of the importance of being content in spite of any and all circumstances. Philippians 4:11-13 says:

> I am not saying this because I am in need, for I have learned to be content whatever the circumstances. I know what it is to be in need, and I know what

it is to have plenty. I have learned the secret of being content in any and every situation, whether well fed or hungry, whether living in plenty or in want. I can do all this through him who gives me strength.

Note that Paul stresses that contentment is a learned behavior. No one is born with the skill of contentment, nor is it easy to develop due to our human nature, but Paul shows that it is possible.

At this point, you are possibly thinking seriously of taking this book back to wherever you got it and asking for your money back. You may be thinking, "I bought this book to learn how to get a better job, and this guy is chastising me for even looking." Well, that's not exactly what I'm saying. It's just that I have seen so many people spend tons of time and emotional energy on a job search without thinking seriously and discussing with others why they even want a change. I promise that the book will address how to conduct a successful job search. But I can't endorse going down that path without providing some insight into how to avoid ending up as I did in Chapter one.

I spent a lot of years "always on the lookout" for my next job. Earlier in my career, I was accused more than once of being a professional job changer, which, quite frankly, was almost true at times. Even when I was in a great job, I spent hours a week looking at the company's job bulletin board. I'd often spend time planting seeds with others that I was the best candidate for a job, not knowing if it would even interest me. So trust me when I say I'm an expert in the perils of frivolous job searching.

There are several risks that come with "just looking" on a regular basis. First, it is far too easy to lose focus on the job you are currently being paid to do. More than once, I've caught myself slacking on my paying job because I was so focused on finding a better one. Never forget that one of the most powerful tools in finding a new job is having good references. You can't afford to get a reputation of being slack. Second, as long as you are looking, you will be convincing yourself that there are better jobs out there for you and that you should be getting more respect and making more money, both of which, frankly, may or may not be true.

So, should everyone simply suck it up, be content, and stay in the job they are in forever? Absolutely not. I'm merely suggesting that you take a hard look at how blessed you are, where you are right now, and prayerfully consider the possibility that it might be the right place at this point in time. Or maybe you should have left where you are five years ago.

I don't know whether or not you should embark on a job search, but God does. Have you asked him? If you have and you know he is endorsing your search for a change, then get going. If you aren't sure, then stick with the job you are in until you've checked things out with God. Commit to pray for his insight for a while. He'll let you know. Why not start right now and pray this prayer below:

> *Dear Lord, I know you love me and want and know what is best for me. In your Word, you are clear that you will be generous in providing wisdom if we ask. Please still my mind and show me your will for my career. Amen.*

While I believe most of us need to learn a lot about being content where we are, I am equally sure that God is calling many of us to listen to his plan and make a change. Perhaps he wants you to spend more of your time in direct ministry for him. Maybe he wants you to find a job that allows you to spend more time being there for your family. What about the gifts and graces with which he has blessed you? Are they becoming stagnant from non-use? Maybe he has a big plan for you ten years from now and having a new job now will prepare you for that time of increase and blessing. It might even be that there is one person in another company who needs you as a friend. Is that a frivolous reason to make a job change? Not if it's God's plan. So often we make everything all about ourselves. Me, me, me! But as Christians, we are called to serve—not only to serve God, but to serve others, too.

What are God's reasons for wanting you to make a change? I don't know. Actually, you don't have to know why, either. All you really have to be sure of is that you are seeking his will for your career, not your own will.

> **Lesson: If you are struggling to figure out what you want to do with your life, I have good news. It's not your job to "figure it out." God already has (Jeremiah 29:11).**

It's your job to listen... As Jeremiah so boldly points out in Jeremiah 29:11, God already knows the plans he has for you. He knows them because he designed them. All the pressure is on God, not you. The hard part is breaking through the lies you've been taught (often with good intentions) and learned from the way the world works. Sometimes we need to do a reset and start with a blank piece of paper. I am confident that many people are completely missing what God wants them to do. On the other hand, many people are exactly where God wants them, but they are not content because they don't realize it.

I know what you are thinking now. Enough philosophy. How do I get started?

CHAPTER 3

Why Do I Need a Job?

Why do you need a job? When I ask most people that question (and I ask it a lot), the response is typically something between the look a dog gives you when you make a funny noise, and a blunt, "That's a dumb question." I think it is an important question. It should form the foundation of your career search. Some of the answers I've gotten have been:

- I just lost my job.
- I have to feed my family.
- I feel like I can do so much more.
- My current job is a dead end.
- I hate what I'm doing.
- I need more money.
- I'm just not happy where I am.
- I can't explain it; I just don't feel like I'm in the right place.
- I want to find something before they lay me off.

There are many variations of the above, as well as many I haven't mentioned. They all seem pretty normal, don't they? Would you respond to anyone who gave one of these responses, "Are you crazy? That's no reason to leave a job"? Probably not. However, this is where I would like to throw a wrench in the gears. Just for a moment, let's suppose that there are only two valid reasons for looking for a new job. That would be a good thing, wouldn't it? Simple principles are always the best. While I claim no authority here, I would like to suggest the following hypothesis:

There are only two valid reasons for beginning an active job search.

1. I am currently unable to provide the basic needs (food and shelter) for my family and me.

2. God is leading me somewhere else.

What's your reaction to that? Did I leave anything out? Are there other valid reasons? I find it uncomfortable to suggest the above. It is an extremely bold proposition. However, from my personal experience, a job search not motivated by one or both of these two factors, tends to be significantly more difficult, and the results are often not in our best interest.

Note to those who are currently without a job: The next several paragraphs are about looking for a job while you already have one. I encourage you not to skip this section. There are truths in this section that apply to everyone, and I believe that understanding this may help protect you from troubles once you are employed.

At this point, I feel it is important to address a common mantra in the work world. Many people say, "I'm always on the lookout for something better." That makes sense, right? That's a prudent thing to do, isn't it? It depends. Let me restate "I'm always on the lookout for something better" in a different way. What I think many of us really mean by this statement is, "I'm never going to be content in my current situation." OUCH! That hits me right between the eyes. I've found myself in that place many, many times. While I generally "catch myself" going down that path, more often than not, it isn't long before I am sliding down that slippery slope again.

In my first fifteen years of work, I changed jobs quite a bit within one large company. My friends joked with me that I was a "professional job changer." It was true. Within six months of most new jobs, I was already spending significant time thinking about or trying to find what I would do next. I always felt like I was on a treadmill, trying to find the "perfect job" for me. I even sometimes brought God into the mix and told myself, "God wants me to be happy. If

I'm not happy, then God must want me in a different job." It took more years than I'm comfortable admitting for me to realize that part of what God was trying to teach me was to be content wherever he had me at the time.

There is one other concern I have with the "I'm always looking for something better" mindset.

> **Lesson: Finding a job is HARD WORK. It takes a tremendous amount of time and energy. If you are really in job search mode, it's like having another full-time job.**

One of the problems a restless mindset caused throughout my career was that my job searches often took me away from the things I was supposed to be doing for the job I already had and was being paid to do. I was sometimes cheating my current employer. That definitely goes against God's Word.

> **Lesson: A job search should have a clear starting point and ending point.**

That lesson sounds straightforward, but let me take it one step further. I will suggest that there are two valid starting points for a job search:

1. I am not currently able to provide the basic needs of myself and my family.

2. In diligent prayer and devotion to God, He has revealed to me that it is time to begin a job search.

When a job comes out of nowhere

It is important to note that there is a variation of the second point. I will never claim to be able to explain how God works. I do know, however, that there are times when he works quickly and with complete disregard for the processes we would like to follow. That's exciting! God's timing is important to mention because there are times when someone is not searching at all, and suddenly a new job opportunity will appear. When that happens, we should have only one concern. We must determine whether God endorses that opportunity. Don't respond to the opportunity until you take the time to seek his will. If you sincerely want to know his will, he will reveal it.

All unexpected job opportunities are not blessings from God. Many are temptations to lead us farther away from him. We can't allow ourselves to rush into making a decision about something so important. Our choices not only affect us, but they also impact our families. Our choices also influence our Christian walk. If our motivation for wanting a new job is ego-based, we are allowing the enemy to draw us into the trap of conceit. Sometimes we are far better off not accepting a glamorous or high-profile job that strokes our egos. Think of it not as turning down a dream job, but as refusing the enemy's temptation. I know what you are thinking. "John! Are you insane? Are you telling me that if a great job falls into my lap I shouldn't take it before someone else does?"

That is not what I'm saying at all. What I am saying is that you shouldn't take it until you are confident God will bless the move. God will honor the fact that you make him an integral part of the process.

One of the many things I've learned about myself during my many job searches is this. Once an offer is on the table, my ego engages, and I am ready to say yes. The simple fact that someone wants to pay me money and has chosen me over others to help their firm stirs up the worst in me. I am a person who thrives on approval and recognition. I'm not proud of it, but it is true. I have a difficult time saying no to anything when someone is stroking my ego. Knowing that, I've developed a tactic that works well for me.

Whenever I sense that a job search begins to go well, my prayer is this:

WHY DO I NEED A JOB?

Lord, you know me. You know that once my ego is stroked, I tend to sprint forward without thinking. I know that I am not strong enough to say 'no' to this opportunity, should it be offered. If this opportunity is against your will, make it so clear to me that I cannot say "yes."

A wise and dear friend shared the following awesome nugget with me more than fifteen years ago.

Lesson: "Push on every door you see, but don't kick on it."

If you are continually seeking God's will, the doors will open easily, and you should walk through. If they don't, do not try to force the door open. That wisdom has served me extremely well over the years, including in many non-work scenarios.

Here is the bottom line:

Before you begin to exert your energy on a job search, have a solid answer for why you need another job.

I would like to wrap up this chapter with a brief story about a conversation I had recently with a gentleman. We'll call him Bob.

I had known Bob for more than ten years. Although I didn't know him extremely well, we were friends. He is a great guy and obviously tremendously bright and gifted in business.

Bob contacted me at home one evening and said he wanted to meet with me about "finding work." Someone had told him that I helped people with that. I told him I would be glad to meet with him, and we scheduled a time for coffee the following week. When the time came for our meeting, I started with my normal line of questions.

"Why are we here?" is usually where I start. He explained that he had been out of work for a while and was becoming extremely frustrated at the lack of results in his job search. The next question I ask tends to catch people off guard. "Are you OK financially right now? Are you able to provide for your family?" I ask this, not to be nosy, but if I am to truly help, I need to understand the "why" behind a job search as well as the seeker's sense of urgency for finding a new job.

Bob's answer caught *me* off guard. He smiled kindly and explained, in an almost apologetic tone, that his family had been blessed financially. They had money coming in from several sources, had very little debt, and had the ability to liquidate assets if they needed to. I was relieved to hear his answer. At this point, I understood that there was no real financial sense of urgency, and my line of questioning changed.

It is probably important at this point for me to inform you that I start all job search counseling sessions by asking for permission to be extremely blunt. So far everyone has said "absolutely." I'm not sure what I'll do if someone ever says, "No, John, I really need you to be subtle." I'll likely end the meeting and refer them to someone else!

My next question to Bob, who appeared to be in his late forties to early fifties was, "Do you even need a job at all?" He said he did. I asked him why. While I hope I didn't let it show, his response nearly knocked me off my chair. He said, "I need a job so that I can have a purpose." I honestly didn't know whether to scream at him or to put my head on the table and weep.

I knew Bob had a family member in his home who had been battling serious illness for several years. While he had been out of work, he had been able to be there and provide great care for his family.

The good news in this case is that Bob was already taking care of his family to the best of his ability. Being the direct, confrontational guy God created me to be, I said to him, "is it possible that your purpose right now is to be with your family, and you should put the job search on the back-burner for now?" He said yes, but went on to give me more details regarding what he wanted in a job, and how great it made him feel to have people at work who needed his expertise. I do not know for sure whether it was in God's plan for Bob to find a new job right then. That's not my place. I suggested that he stop his search and get an answer before he went any further.

I want to give a word of caution here. In reading the above story, it will be easy to jump to the conclusion that Bob was a bad guy. Not the case at all. Put in the same scenario, I'm pretty sure many people, including me, would have felt the same way.

I cannot emphasize strongly enough how much damage I believe Satan is doing in the world by "messing up" our view of work and our jobs. We tend to get most, if not all, of our views and beliefs about work from the secular world.

A quick search, using an online Bible, shows no less than 500 verses that mention "work." Yet, unfortunately, it is rare that we talk about "work" at church. I encourage you to do some reading and research about God's view of work.

An excellent read on the subject is Doug Spada's book *Monday Morning Atheist*.[1] In this great, inspired book, Doug addresses the fact that Christians often turn God off on Monday morning when they go to their jobs.

While I won't list all 500+ verses here, below are a few selections you should consider. Hopefully, they will make you think and will provide encouragement for you to dig deeper

WHY DO I NEED A JOB? 33

into the topic. It's a pretty long list. Please don't rush through it. If you can't do it now, please set aside a time to meditate on these words and ask God to speak to you through them.

> Proverbs 14:23: All hard work brings a profit, but mere talk leads only to poverty.

> Proverbs 18:9: One who is slack in his work is brother to one who destroys.

> Matthew 20:13: But he answered one of them, "Friend, I am not being unfair to you. Didn't you agree to work for a denarius?"

> Luke 5:5: Simon answered, "Master, we've worked hard all night and haven't caught anything. But because you say so, I will let down the nets."

> John 5:17: Jesus said to them, "My Father is always at his work to this very day, and I, too, am working."

> 2 Corinthians 9:8: And God is able to make all grace abound to you, so that in all things at all times, having all that you need, you will abound in every good work.

> Ephesians 4:28: He who has been stealing must steal no longer, but must

work, doing something useful with his own hands, that he may have something to share with those in need.

Colossians 3:23: Whatever you do, work at it with all your heart, as working for the Lord, not for men.

1 Thessalonians 2:9: Surely you remember, brothers, our toil and hardship; we worked night and day in order not to be a burden to anyone while we preached the gospel of God to you.

1 Thessalonians 4:11: Make it your ambition to lead a quiet life, to mind your own business and to work with your hands, just as we told you.

Hebrews 13:17: Obey your leaders and submit to their authority. They keep watch over you as men who must give an account. Obey them so that their work will be a joy, not a burden, for that would be of no advantage to you.

My original list had more than twenty additional scripture references in it. I whittled the list down to those I thought were the most pertinent to our discussion. I pray that you will keep them nearby and refer to them often. God's word is much more important and accurate than mine!

CHAPTER 4

"What Do You Do?"

Have you ever noticed how prominent that question is in our society? "What do you do?" It has almost become the universal greeting for social events and gatherings. The conversations go like this.

"Hi, I'm John Freeze."

"Hi John, nice to meet you. What do you do?"

"I'm Director of Sales for a technology company, how about you?"

"I'm VP of Logistics for LMNOP Company."

Just once, I'd like to have the guts to respond more appropriately. Something like this would be cool.

"Hi, I'm John Freeze."

"Hi John, nice to meet you. What do you do?"

"Well, I struggle daily to understand how God wants me to spend my time. Even when I catch a glimpse, I have a difficult time being obedient for more than a day or so. I try to spend as much time as possible loving my family and providing them with guidance, but that, too, is a great challenge. I also am spending quite a bit of time in prayer these days. Our pastor and I are discussing the formation of a prayer ministry at our church, but we really aren't sure where the Lord is leading us."

"Heeyyy...umm....thanks for sharing that, John. I need to get something to drink. I'm sure we'll catch up later."

Why is it that our society puts so much emphasis on our job, our title, and the company for which we work? There are other books written on that subject, I'm sure. I don't understand the why. But I do know that it is true. Far too often we define others and ourselves based on where we work, what our title is, what upward opportunity we have before us, how much money we make...and the list goes on and on.

"WHAT DO YOU DO?"

I was caught completely off-guard recently, and it made me realize how often I have fallen prey to this trap. I was sitting at a table with a group of six other men whom I didn't know. I am not much on starting conversations. I'm extremely introverted, but the silence was more than I could stand. I turned to the man beside me and started to say, "What do you do?" When the words were right on the edge of my lips, I stopped. I wiped the sweat from my brow and leaned back in my chair. You see, I was having dinner in our church gym with the men who were staying at our church's homeless ministry that night. The other six men at the table had not only no jobs, but no homes. I was stumped. I didn't know how to show interest in them because I couldn't ask, "What do you do?" or "Where do you live?" Those are my solid crutches for conversation starters.

I learned more things that night sleeping among the homeless than I can explain. But two truths are relevant here.

- We start too many conversations with "What do you do?"

- As the night went on and I spoke to these men, I did get to know them. I had an enormous amount of respect and love for them when they walked out of our church the next morning. And they had no jobs! It wasn't about their jobs. They had an awesome identity without one.

Some of you may be about to jump out of your skin, being this far into a book on job search without getting any networking or resume tips (I promise it is coming!), but this is the most important thing I believe I can share with you.

> **Lesson: You are not defined by your job (or the lack of one). You are defined by your Holy Father, who created you in his image.**

Pause to allow this lesson to sink in for a moment. God makes it clear in his Word that he created each of us in his image. Combine that with the fact that Jesus would have died for you even if you were the only one ever created. He didn't die just for "all the world." He died specifically for you.

Let that percolate within your heart and mind... Think about it... Meditate on it... Now answer the question. "What do you do?"

CHAPTER 5

Your Resume – Telling Others About Your Skills and Experiences

OK. Finally! Some real tactical job search stuff. Let's talk about resumes and how we describe our strengths to others.

The first thing I want to say about resumes is that I don't like them. Sorry. I'm sure that isn't what you wanted to hear. You see, my current job is in sales, but in the two jobs I've held where my primary responsibility was staffing, I reviewed thousands of resumes. I know; "thousands" sounds like a big exaggeration, but I've checked the figures, and it is an accurate number. For about four years, my primary role was to find candidates for job openings in my company, interview them, get them in front of the hiring manager for interviews, help with the selection process, and, finally, to notify those who weren't selected, and to negotiate job offers with those who were.

A resume is a piece of paper. I think so much emphasis is put on resumes, not because it is the most important thing, but because it is the easiest part of a job search to discuss. There are tons and tons of information out there on resumes, and much of it is valid. I won't go into my personal preferences on format and what the best resumes should and shouldn't contain. That would only be my opinion, and it is unlikely that I will be reviewing your resume. However, I will share with you some of my overall thoughts on resumes.

1. Resumes serve only two purposes:

    a. To summarize everything you know and have done into one or two pages to make reviewing your qualifications easy on the person responsible for selecting interview candidates, and

    b. To provide a guide for determining the questions asked during an interview.

Especially in today's difficult job market, there tend to be numerous candidates for most job openings. I've heard recent stories from hiring managers of receiving hundreds of resumes for one single opening. Many large companies use resume databases with key word searches. Whether or not your resume gets pulled for consideration often depends upon the somewhat random search terms that the person querying the database uses. Again, there are many books and articles on writing the best resumes. It would be a good idea to check a few of those out. But DON'T

YOUR RESUME 41

spend more than 20% of the time you have allotted to job search on working on your resume because…

2. Almost no one gets hired because of their resume.

Refer to fact #1. The purpose of a resume is not to get a job. A resume's purpose is to generate an interview.

3. There are very few ways to differentiate yourself in a resume, assuming your resume even gets read.

I'm not trying to be harsh, but do not assume that every resume sent in for a position gets read. I can tell you that there were days that I "reviewed" hundreds of resumes. Do you think I read them all and considered what the person might really be like? I wish I could tell you I did, but the truth is, many went straight to be scanned in the database without human eyes ever seeing them. Instead of really reading them, I looked for something to stand out. What stood out for me?

4. Very few resumes list anything quantifiable or specific about a person's experience.

Please allow me to be blunt. When I read a resume that has a bulleted item that reads:

- Coordinated events for the southern region sales department

Several questions come to mind:

- How many events did you coordinate?
- Did anyone attend the events?
- Did the events go well? Were they successful?
- If deemed successful, what does that mean?
- What does "coordinated" mean? Were you responsible for logistics? Did you really just arrange travel?
- Did you create an agenda and its content? Were you the one who had to identify and recruit presenters?

You get the idea. If you didn't give any of those details, my assumption is "it didn't go well." Is that fair? Nope. But it's real.

Be specific and use numbers if at all possible. For example, what if the bullet list above read like this:

- Led a team of five in developing and implementing an event with a $26,000 budget that:

- Had 350 attendees
- Brought professional speakers in from six Fortune 100 companies
- Provided an experience that reinforced the company's focus to "have fun while getting it done"
- Achieved survey results of "exceeded my expectations" from 83% of attendees

You see, when you are writing your resume, you already know what you mean. The person reading it knows absolutely nothing about what you have done, other than what you put in writing.

Be as clear and as detailed as possible, without being too long. Given the space constraints, clarity and brevity present an enormous challenge, but they are critical to the process. Three- or four-page resumes just won't be read. I have known recruiters and assistants for executives in some firms who have told me that "if it is more than two pages it goes in the trash." You are better off to provide more detail about fewer activities in your previous work than to list lots of things with no detail. There are some who will disagree with me, but that is my opinion.

Note: An exception to the two-page rule is if you are applying for a true executive level opportunity. In many cases, there will be a retained search firm representing you in that situation. They will often be doing an extensive write-up on your behalf.

5. **A purpose statement/objective on a resume is a positive thing only if you are going to be willing to re-write it for every specific job for which you apply.**

Objectives at the beginning of a resume tend to fall into three groups.

   a. They are generic and have no impact on the reader.

   b. They are specific, but don't match the exact job for which the reader is considering you.

   c. They are well tailored to the opportunity for which you are being considered.

Point a) above needs little explanation. I can tell you that I read more than my share of "I'm a results-oriented team player looking for the opportunity to leverage my diverse skills in a rewarding company where I can grow and assist the company in its mission." (If there were a universal symbol for vomit, I would insert it here). If it isn't specific, why waste the space on the paper with it? Omit extraneous wording and use the space you free up by adding more CONCRETE details demonstrating how awesome your work has been.

On the other hand, I've also seen specific objectives like this:

"I am looking for an opportunity to continue to develop my skills as a project manager in the mechanical engineering field while pursuing my Project Management Institute certifications."

That sounds great, right? Well, maybe. But what if that resume ends up in the hands of a hiring manager in the IT department? Everything about your resume looks perfect to her. You have all the right skills, even went to her favorite college, which seems to be where all the best project managers are educated. When she looks back over your resume for the second time and reads "develop my skills as a project manager in the mechanical engineering field," she may immediately jump to the conclusion that *this person wouldn't be interested in a job in the IT department.* Hence, you don't get a call for an interview. Sounds harsh, but I've seen similar circumstances happen many times.

So, are you frustrated now? You thought you would start by writing a good resume, and now you don't know where to start? I'm hoping the answer is "yes" to that last question.

> **Lesson: Writing a resume is NOT the first step in conducting a job search.**

A lot of folks send their friends to me to talk about "finding a job." Nearly always, when I meet the job seeker, they want to start out by handing their resume to me. It is rare that I ever look at it.

It's just not the most important aspect of job searching, and I know that I have nothing unique to offer them about resumes. As I mentioned before, there are tons and tons of good guides, books, classes, and instructors who will help you with that.

So what is the first step? The most important thing to do is to take an inventory of your abilities, strengths, the kind of work you like to do, and the areas about which you are passionate. Then practice how to explain that to people.

Many people think they can rely on their resume alone to tell people about their strengths and what they do. While a resume helps with that, you need to be able to explain your strengths and passions in much greater detail when speaking with someone.

One of the bad habits we tend to have is that when someone asks, "What do you do?" we answer with a job title.

"Hi Mary, what do you do?"

"I'm an accountant."

That's pretty straight forward. Now you know what Mary does. Or do you? There are many kinds of accounting professionals. Some accountants audit tax returns; others might manage people or handle contract work, and there are accountants who are consultants on accounting processes. I knew an "accountant" who ran Operations for the IT department for a

Fortune 100 firm. By the way, he was GREAT at it.

What we need to answer about ourselves is something like this.

If I look back over all the jobs I've had, both paid and volunteer, what was I doing when I was having the most fun and being the most productive?

When I went down this line of questioning with a friend, he started with, "I'm the CFO of a small business." Thirty minutes later we ended with, "the thing I really like most about my job is purchasing and working with vendors on contracts."

If he had gone down a path in search of a job as a CFO for another small company, he might never have had the opportunity to work with purchasing again.

The questions you should begin trying to answer are:

> ➢ There have been times in my life (work-related and not) that I have felt extremely energized and productive. I was "in the zone." Reflecting on those times, what did they have in common? Was I using similar skills, even though the jobs may have been completely different?

- What do others most frequently depend on me to do?

- What can I do better than most others?

- If someone really wants to leverage me to the fullest in a job, they need to make sure that I am spending a significant amount of my time working on _____ (fill in the blank)

- I tend to be most effective when I am _____. (fill in the blank).

- What are the unique gifts God has given to me?

These questions only scratch the surface. Knowing the answers is important, and the effort is worthy of your time to pursue it. Answering these questions will help keep you from getting another job as an engineer, for example, when the truth is you hate details, but you have an engineering degree.

There are lots of resources available out there to help with uncovering your strengths. One of my favorites is the book, *Strengthfinder 2.0* by Tom Rath.[2] I still use this resource to keep myself in check, trying to ensure that I'm engaged in activities that align with my strengths.

There are two enormous benefits you will gain from thoroughly completing the exercise Rath suggests.

First, you will quickly realize that there are significantly more job opportunities that are a great fit for you than you thought.

Second, the likelihood of enjoying and thriving in the next job you enter goes up tremendously!

If you came up with a set of strengths and passions and realized "there aren't many jobs that would fully leverage this," I have two pieces of advice for you.

1. Get creative. Talk to others. Research and read. AND PRAY about it. There may be jobs you have never even heard of that would perfectly leverage your skills.

2. Consider the fact that the main purpose for your "job" may be to provide income, and you should be searching for volunteer areas to engage those passions and strengths for God's Kingdom.

This next statement will seem counterintuitive, so prepare yourself. No knee-jerk reactions, please.

For some people, I believe it is ok that the job they are in doesn't necessarily leverage their greatest strengths.

Something that I struggled a great deal with earlier in my career, and still do at times, is whether or not I should be in full-time ministry.

I believe that for some people, their paying job is a means of paying the bills, and their greater calling may be in volunteering during their non-work hours. It doesn't have to be a "paid ministry" to be a real ministry!

While being in the right job is important, make sure you accept this powerful truth:

God loves you so much that he sent his son to die for you. That fact does not change, based on the job you have. Your worth to the Lord is NOT connected to your job, or to the fact that you don't have one!

CHAPTER 6

Whom Can You Trust?

At this point, I am going to reveal to you the key to a successful career search. It's not a networking tip. It's not a new resume format. It is a TRUTH from God's word.

Proverbs 3:5-6 says "Trust in the Lord with all your heart and lean not on your own understanding. In all your ways acknowledge him and he will make your paths straight."

My guess is that you have likely heard these verses many times before. What in the world does this Scripture have to do with a job search? In a word, everything. Let's break it down.

"Trust in the Lord with all your heart." On the surface, that sounds simple. Well, consider this question. Do you worry? Ever? About anything? Do you worry that you won't find a job or perhaps that you won't find the right job? I remember hearing a long time ago that worry is a sin. That really bothered me. I had to put some serious thought into it. I came up with only four reasons we worry.

1. We don't think God can handle our situation. (We don't think he is big enough, strong enough, or powerful enough).

2. We don't trust that God wants what's best for us.

3. We don't think we can handle the situation.

4. We are inclined to be negative and to worry.

Let's look at each of these in some detail.

1. We don't think God can handle our situation.

Many of us have not truly accepted the fact that God is omnipotent. Sure, we've read the Bible stories, we sing the songs about his power, but we never fully embrace the fact that he can do anything. A large part of our undoing here is that we subconsciously buy into the line of thinking that goes something like this. "If he is truly all powerful, there would be no problems. And there are certainly lots of problems in the world and in my life." Again, I don't believe we actually go through that logic, but we don't see "proof" that he is all powerful. Christians significantly wiser and more studied than I am have written volumes on "why bad things happen." I won't claim to be a theologian. But I would like to point out a few truths from the Bible that can help us overcome this false mindset.

God created everything.

I was recently speaking to a close friend regarding a common business issue with which he and a Christian co-worker were struggling. I challenged him to invite the co-worker to pray with him. When my friend told me a day later that he hadn't asked the fellow to pray with him about it, I asked why. His response was a common one. He said, "I'm nervous."

(It is important here to point out that I have been told I have "the tact of a rope burn.") My response was, "So what you are telling me is that you don't believe that the God who was able to create the universe is powerful enough to protect you while you ask a fellow Christian to pray with you?" Most people laugh at that story (except the guy who was part of it). But isn't it true for all of us? Don't we worry only when we forget to stop and remind ourselves how much more powerful God is than we are? Spend time meditating on God's power.

Some scriptures to consider are:

> Genesis Chapter 1: This chapter tells how God created everything. Look at the world

around you and the people in your life. God created every cell, atom, and molecule. If God is powerful enough to create the entire universe, doesn't it stand to reason that he can handle something as mundane as a job search? We are only a tiny part of God's creation, but he tells us we are the apple of his eye (Psalm 17:8). He loves us so much he sent his only Son to die for our sins. Regardless of our situation, God is more than able to handle everything.

> Take away: As Creator of heaven and earth, God can create the perfect job for you. It's time to entrust your job search to him.

➤ Exodus Chapter 15: The words written in this chapter are amazing. Do we truly believe that God is powerful enough to shatter our enemies with one hand (Exodus 15:6)? Do you see God as able to move oceans with his breath, or do you doubt his ability to help find, or create, a job for you?

> Take away: You must decide whether you will trust God and take him at his word or continue to try and handle everything yourself. If you truly believe what this scripture teaches, you have to do your part in finding a job while allowing him to shatter any doubts you have or move oceans of fear out of the way.

➢ Psalm 97: This has become one of my favorite scriptures in recent years. My view of God was, and often still is, much too wimpy. This chapter provides a vivid picture of power. While it is of utmost importance that we understand the depth of God's love, it is equally important that we do not lose sight of his awesome power. Do you believe that "fire goes before him and consumes his foes on every side" (Psalm 97:3)?

> Take away: The very nature of fire clears a path. God can open up a pathway to your dream job. Allow God's fire to burn up any hindrances your own efforts might be causing. God's promises are not only powerful, but they are true. He will do what he says he will do. Will you do what he is asking you to do and simply trust him?

After reading each of these, we honestly have three choices.

1. We can accept the truths in God's Word and the fact that God's power is beyond our comprehension. Whether we comprehend or believe it or not, he can handle anything. Especially a job search! or…

2. We can reject these precepts and choose not to believe the scriptures, or…

3. We can be lulled to sleep thinking "but those kinds of things don't happen now. God is different now."

I have chosen #1. You must choose for yourself.

2. We don't trust that God wants the best for us.

That can't be right, can it? He sent his only son to die for us. Of course, we *say* we believe he wants the best for us. *But do we really believe?* Let's dig into it a bit. Have you ever known for sure that God was calling you to do something (large or small) and you "wimped out." Why didn't you follow through? I can only speak for myself, but I wimp out more often than I'll choose to share. Why? Because as we say in the South, "I'm skeered." Fear—that roadblock that ties our hands and feet—renders us powerless, frozen in time and space, and too afraid to take any action. What causes my fear? It could be anything, but for me it often comes down to being afraid of how I might be perceived by someone in the near term. A common word for this is PRIDE! I don't usually go through a thought process and come to the conclusion that "this is not God's will," and I rarely determine that in the long-run, it won't be "good" or have a positive impact. I get stuck on HOW IT WILL MAKE ME FEEL RIGHT NOW. There are multiple problems with this concept.

First, I understand more and more every day that it should have nothing to do with how I feel. I haven't found in the Word where God promised to make us feel good. As a matter of fact, those in scripture who were obedient often suffered greatly. We don't like that. We've bought into the lie that "success" = "feeling good."

Second, our reference of time in making many decisions is ridiculous. Let me give you an example. I made it up, but similar things have happened to most of us hundreds of time.

I'm walking with my kids on the street of a busy city, shopping for the holidays. We walk past a man sitting in a wheelchair, holding out a tin can for change. My kids look up at me with that look they have. I stop, reach in my pocket and pull out a few bucks. I put them in the can. The Spirit prompts me to offer to pray with the man. But I don't. Why? Because I don't know what to pray? No, that's not the issue. Because I'm "afraid" of the man? No, it's a busy street with lots of folks around, and he's handicapped. Because I don't believe in the power of prayer? No way. I could write another book on personal stories where I've seen the results of prayer. So what's the problem? I cringe when I give you the honest answer. I'm driven not to pray by the power of an emotion that says "I'll feel uncomfortable." Someone I know from work might walk by. What would they think if they saw me like that? The man might say no to my request to pray for him. Regarding outcomes, the time frame I've considered is about 48 seconds!

What if I had a larger time horizon for considering the results. Lots of things could happen.

- My kids might remember the incident when they are faced with similar circumstances ten years later. (In truth, knowing my kids, they'd jump right in and pray with me).

- The man could have been praying for a sign that God is real, and God might want to use my obedience in prayer to change the man's entire life.

- Someone from work might see me and come to me a month later and ask me

WHOM CAN YOU TRUST? 59

"what was that all about?" Perhaps an act of obedience might encourage them to react differently if faced with a similar situation.

Although I've admitted that I'm no philosopher or theologian, I think there is a principle that following a prompting of the Spirit could be extremely uncomfortable in the near-term, but in God's time, he will always be glorified through our obedience. Unfortunately, I allow the risk of near-term discomfort to dictate my response. In short, I have no Kingdom view in the situation, only a view of how it might be a negative for me right now.

I buy into the lie that says "if it's good for me, it has to feel good." Hogwash. The Bible tells us that is not so. In 1 Peter 4:12-13, the apostle Peter writes:

> Dear friends, do not be surprised at the painful trial you are suffering, as though something strange were happening to you. But rejoice that you participate in the sufferings of Christ, so that you may be overjoyed when his glory is revealed.

So rather than focusing on a momentary suffering, we should consider the bigger picture. As humans, we often assume that everything is all about us, but sometimes God wants to use us for the benefit of others.

3. We don't think we can handle the situation.

Doubt might be the primary reason we worry. The good news is that our premise is often correct on this one. We can't handle the situation. The issue is that we even consider the notion that we are supposed to "handle the situation." As a little boy, I remember singing a song, "Jesus Loves Me."[3] The lyrics said, "Little ones to him belong. They are weak, but he is strong." I wish there were a second verse to that song reminding us that "big ones to him belong." For some reason, as we grow in stature and intellect, we unconsciously change the words of the song to "I am strong so I'll just call on him when things are really bad." We are weak. He is strong. Will we ever get that through our heads? We are only strong when we allow his strength to work through us.

(If you are starting to question what this has to do with job search, PLEASE don't check out on me yet. Trusting in God and depending upon his strength are too fundamental to the issue.)

4. We are inclined to be negative and to worry.

Again, for a detailed discussion concerning negativity and worry, I will defer to some of the incredible Christian authors who have written and preached about these subjects, but I will make a general statement that I am confident is true.

God created man in his image, and with that fact comes our enormous capacity for hope and confidence in the future.

Spiritual warfare is a reality, and I believe that one of the most active strategies of the enemy is to, bit by bit, piece by piece, day by day, turn us all into pessimists. Are you predisposed to think things probably will NOT be ok? Perhaps you are. I have been at times in my life. Doubt and fear are the enemy's lies. We might suffer severe pain and hardship but we must be absolutely sold out on the truth that God wins in the end, and so do we. When we are negative, it is because we are focused on the problem, not on our awesome God. Max Lucado's book *Facing Your Giants* is a wonderful testament to this. Lucado says, "See your struggle as God's canvas. On it he will paint his multicolored supremacy."[4]

If you are negative, you are leaning on someone other than the God who created the universe for your solutions.

Now, back to job search. The key to straightening the path for your job search is right there in Proverbs 3:5. Trust in the Lord with all your heart and lean not on your own understanding. I'm not trying to beat you down here, but please be honest with yourself. This Scripture does not suggest simply telling people that you trust in the Lord. It is a command to do it! It also doesn't say trust in the Lord only when you can't figure it out on your own. It says DO NOT lean on your own understanding. In theory, the premise for this book is quite simple.

> *Trust God with your job search and don't try to figure it out yourself. Don't worry about it. God will take care of it.*

In practice, "letting go and letting God" goes against most everything the world has ever taught.

I strongly encourage you to reread this chapter and pray for God to reveal to you the ways in which you are not fully trusting Him. Don't rush through it. I pray that you will take this step seriously and will come to grips with the reality of your current situation and that you will fully see and accept the truth: God is forever and always trustworthy and is crying out for you to believe that and act like it!

CHAPTER 7

Everyone Needs a Sherpa to Keep Them on the Path

Now go do something!

Get ready, because now is the time for the proverbial drumroll. I've spent over half the book telling you stories and telling you what not to do! The part you've been waiting on is finally here. It is time for me to tell you what I believe you should do in order to have a successful job search.

Let's look at the second part of that awesome word in Proverbs. Chapter 3 verse 6 says:

> In all your ways acknowledge him and he will make your paths straight.

Don't freak out on me here, but I have another counterintuitive truth for you regarding the job search process.

The things you do in the process are not nearly as important as how you do them and whom you ask for help. What does that mean in the real world? Some examples:

- The format you use to build your resume isn't important. However, acknowledging that God is the source of the gifts and talents you have is vital.

- Whether you wear a blue shirt with a red tie or a white shirt with a yellow tie, or a black turtleneck to the interview isn't important. Stopping before you walk into an interview and asking God for guidance, peace, and discernment during the upcoming conversation is imperative.

- Whether you go to the career fair today instead of spending time looking for a job on Monster.com isn't that important. Staying in communion with the Lord and being obedient to the promptings of the Spirit regarding your search are invaluable.

- Deciding between looking for a job in a large company or a small company may consume hours of your time, but it's not nearly as relevant to a successful job search as finding a group of trustworthy friends who will pray for you during your job search.

In a few more paragraphs, I will outline the major steps in a job search, but every step you make must be blanketed in prayer, in order to obtain the results you want. More importantly, earnest prayer is crucial in obtaining the results God wants for you.

A couple of my friends have adopted a strategy I started employing about ten years ago. Before I walk into an interview, I pray that if the opportunity is not God's will, that I will feel physically sick when the interview is over. Crazy? Testing God? I think the answer to both is, "Absolutely not." Have you read Judges 6:36-40? It's the story of Gideon and the fleece and describes how Gideon asked God for a sign concerning a situation. It's one of my favorite stories in the Bible. If we ask God to show us his will in a situation, he will honor that request.

By now, you understand the lack of importance I place on the exalted resume. On the other end of the spectrum sit prayer, accountability partners, and networking. I am convinced that these are the most powerful tools in the job searcher's toolbox.

While I have dedicated chapter 8 to the important topic of networking, let's spend the remainder of this chapter on the vital topics of prayer and accountability partners.

Why do you need accountability partners?

1. They will keep you honest regarding how you are spending your time during your job search, and they will hold you accountable to the process in this book.

2. They will offer you Godly guidance, including telling you some things that are in your "blind spots." There could be areas that would be difficult for you to realize or recognize without Godly advice from people who know you well.

3. They will agree to be intercessors for you, praying for you throughout the process.

I believe it is important to have more than one accountability partner. While the Holy Spirit should be the first on anyone's list, having more than one other person provides a good set of checks and balances, as some of the guidance you get might not be consistent. It is not important that your accountability partners have read this book (though I am fine with it if you choose to buy them a copy). However, it is VITAL that your accountability partners are

EVERYONE NEEDS A SHERPA 67

Godly men and/or women who understand that their role in the process is intended to be as much or more of a spiritual guide as it is to be a business guide for you.

Let's look at a few scriptures that provide great advice and a few strong warnings about picking the right support network for your job search.

> Jeremiah 9:4: "Beware of your friends; do not trust your brothers. For every brother is a deceiver, and every friend a slanderer.
>
> Luke 21:16: You will be betrayed even by parents, brothers, relatives and friends, and they will put some of you to death.
>
> John 15:13: Greater love has no one than this, that he lay down his life for his friends.
>
> John 15:15: I no longer call you servants, because a servant does not know his master's business. Instead, I have called you friends, for everything that I learned from my Father I have made known to you.
>
> Philippians 4:1: Therefore, my brothers, you whom I love and long for, my joy and crown, that is how you should stand firm in the Lord, dear friends!

1 Peter 2:11: Dear friends, I urge you, as aliens and strangers in the world, to abstain from sinful desires, which war against your soul.

Jude 1:20: But you, dear friends, build yourselves up in your most holy faith and pray in the Holy Spirit.

1 John 4:11: Dear friends, since God so loved us, we also ought to love one another.

The scriptures above came from a search for the word "friend" in the Bible. A summary of the qualities you should seek out when considering accountability partners is below:

- Integrity
- Wisdom
- Trust in God
- Honesty (not afraid to tell you what you NEED to hear)
- Dependability
- Faithfulness (willing to meet with you on a regular basis through the process)
- Dedication as a prayer warrior

It is not vital that this is one of your best friends or a family member. Sometimes, those who are closest to us have a difficult time providing objective feedback. Review Jeremiah 9:4 above for a stronger word on this. I am not telling you not to have a spouse, close friend, or relative as one of your accountability partners. I am saying to check the list above for the main criteria. Selecting your accountability partners should be a serious, prayerful exercise.

CHAPTER 8

Networking – Turns Out the Ugly Truth Can Be a Beautiful Thing!

You have your accountability partners in place, understand why you are on a job search, and have learned how to articulate what you do well. It's time to start networking.

If you are not currently in sales, and perhaps even if you are, your stomach starts to roll and your mouth begins to water when you hear the word networking. Hold back the urge to vomit for just a few minutes. I want to dispel some myths about networking to find a job:

Myth 1: I don't know the right people.

Truth 1: You know a lot more of the "right people" than you think you do.

Myth 2: The chances of me meeting someone who has a job available for me are so low, I shouldn't waste my time networking.

Truth 2: The first part of the myth above actually is true, but the second is not. While it's unlikely that people you know "have a job for you" for which they are personally hiring, many people you know have friends, relatives, or acquaintances who DO "have a job" that might be a great fit for you.

Myth 3: No one is interested in taking the time to find a job for me. Everyone is too busy with their own lives.

Truth 3: Networking is how many job opportunities are identified and obtained. Most people genuinely want to help others, so networking is the perfect vehicle for seeking, and giving, assistance to others.

Myth 4: I'm too shy.

Truth 4: It is much easier than you think to have this discussion, even with someone you don't already know. The key is understanding what you are there to discuss. Asking for a job from a stranger would be awkward even for the most outgoing person. As you will learn in this chapter, that is not what you are supposed to be asking when networking!

Myth 5: Only salespeople network, and I'm not a salesperson.

Truth 5: Most successful people, in any vocation, spend time meeting and learning from people from all walks of life. It is a vital exercise both during and after a successful job search.

Myth 6: Networking has a negative connotation and doing it turns people off.

Truth 6: People are offended when people they don't know or barely know show up out of thin air to get a favor. The vast majority of people (even the ones you haven't met yet) are more than willing to sit down and share their experience and insights with someone who is trying to learn from them.

Ok, I know some of you still think this networking stuff is just not in your DNA. Hang in there. Hearing the details removes some of the pressure.

Deciding with whom to network is one of the main areas that causes stress for people. Most people rack their brain and can only come up with one or two people that they know and believe are "network worthy." The reason for this is that most people think you should network only with people who work for a business that might hire you. You have to cast a much, much broader net than that. An understanding of what you are trying to accomplish with networking will likely put you at ease and help you to realize that there are tons of people you already know with whom you can and should be networking.

There are two primary goals for each networking meeting.

1. Gain new insights that are useful to your job search.
2. Add another person to your team of supporters in the market.

Let's take a closer look at each of these.

What kind of insights could you gain from a networking meeting, other than finding out about a job opening? Here are some examples of things I've personally gleaned from networking meetings:

- Someone who knows you well or that you've worked with before might point out a strength that you never realized you had. Thorough knowledge of your strengths helps you articulate them better, which is huge in the job search.

- You might get insight into a career area you have never considered before, perhaps one that would be a great fit for your passions and skills.

- You gain more "real world" information about a career that you are considering and can determine that it is a great fit, or a terrible fit. Either of those is progress! I recall a personal meeting with a "friend of a friend" who owned a manufacturing company. I have a technical degree and a business degree, and I like leading people. I thought that a plant manager position would be a great fit for my background and skills. During that meeting, I learned a lot about what a plant manager does, and ruled it out completely from my list of possible areas for my next job. That was serious progress. Without that meeting, I likely would have applied to lots of jobs and wasted lots of time pursuing something in which I had no interest.

- You get to practice talking about what you do, what your strengths are, and what you are looking for in a job, with someone who is not interviewing you. It's super practice and will help you gain confidence as you refine your message.

While you would obviously love for each person with whom you network to say, "I have a great job for you right here at my company, and it is available immediately," that is certainly rare. In addition to learning and refining your message and your search, effective networking allows you to launch a successful and credible job search campaign of massive proportion.

Accomplishing something in either area in a single meeting should be considered a successful meeting.

Networking Basics

Once you secure a networking meeting with someone, there are some things to remember. Rather than asking for a "networking meeting," explain that you want to meet and get some advice and learn about personal experiences. Keep the following in mind:

- Be curious. You need to introduce yourself, tell them about your education, skills, and interests, and discuss where you are with your search. But don't forget you are there to learn, not just to ask someone, "Do you know of anything that might be a fit for me?" That almost always results in a short conversation.

- Express how much you would value their advice and ideas and how crucial their input is to your search.

- If the meeting is with someone you know well or someone with whom you have worked before, ask if they would be a reference for you. This point is important because you might need formal references during your job search, but more importantly, it gets people in the frame of mind that you want them to be your advocate in their conversations with others.

- Tell them about your strengths and ask them what careers they know about that might be a good match.

- Explain to them what you have already done and are doing in your journey to find a new job.

- Ask whether they know other people to whom you should be talking. If they say yes, make sure and follow up and get them to introduce you. The way you handle this meeting will make them much more willing to introduce you to others.

- Make sure you follow up on anything they recommended, and let them know you followed up and what the outcome was.

- Be THANKFUL for their time and insight. Follow up with a thank-you note, in an email or by mail, expressing your appreciation for their help.

- Remember that Jesus is the light that should shine from your heart, allowing you to be Jesus to, and see Jesus through, each person you meet. You never know when a divine appointment might be taking place or when the person across the table needs your support. Be as eager to help someone else as you are to receive help.

On a tactical note, I have a strong preference to have network meetings in person when possible. The phone is fine for those folks who aren't in your area, but face to face is best. In addition, I am confident that if you can meet over coffee (or another beverage of choice) or a meal, conversations tend to be longer, richer, and more memorable. I realize this can get expensive quickly. Do not put a financial burden on yourself. Remember, lunch is cheaper than dinner, breakfast is usually cheaper than lunch, and there are cheaper places than Starbucks to grab a cup of joe! This might sound silly, but you might have twenty, thirty, or even more of these meetings. Paying for lunches or even coffee adds up quickly. If you are looking for a job, chances are you are not looking for a way to spend more money.

One final note on why I believe networking is critical to your job searching success. A large percentage of all new jobs are in small businesses that do NOT advertise their job openings. In fact, an ADP National Employment Report released June 2014 stated, "Companies with fewer than 50 employees created 45% of the 188,000 new jobs in June."[5]

It can be devastating to a small firm to make even one bad hire. The best small companies realize this and tend to put a heavy weighting on referrals from co-workers (which may come from their friends…those people with whom you network!). The company for which I currently work was recently named an Inc. 5000 company. We number less than thirty employees and have learned while I've been here that the majority of our best employees have come from referrals from our existing team. Conversely, we have had less than a 20% success rate with those hired through search firms. Hiring people without anyone at the company knowing anything about them is seen as an enormous risk.

I know for many of you reading this, you would be much more comfortable just applying for jobs online and working on your resume, but trust me when I say, "GET OUT THERE AND TALK TO PEOPLE!"

I could tell lots of stories about how networking has resulted in a great job being landed that would have otherwise remained "hidden," but I won't turn this into a 300-page book. However, I will share the most recent story that I have personally witnessed. It is much more common for jobs to be identified and landed this way, so spend a moment considering this story.

1. Our church hired a new youth director.
2. In a conversation at church with my wife, Sharon, the new youth director shared that her boyfriend was looking for a job.
3. Sharon suggested that she talk to me because I "help people with that."
4. I met with the boyfriend for about 60 minutes (never met him before that day). He told me what he was good at and what he was looking for, and he asked for help.
5. I introduced him via email to three or four people whom I knew wouldn't mind spending 30 minutes speaking with him.
6. He reached out to them and was able to set up a meeting with one of them right away.
7. Within three weeks of the meeting we held, which occurred because of a "chance" conversation (i.e., networking), the boyfriend was hired. This true story is a beautiful illustration of the power and importance of networking.

I know you are thinking, "it can't be that simple." I can tell you from experience that it doesn't always happen that quickly, but I can tell you it happens a lot. Personal introductions are powerful in a job search! A couple of other facts about the true story above you should know.

- I had not spoken with the person to whom I introduced the job seeker in about a year. I had not worked with him closely in six or seven years. He trusted my recommendation because of a large deal we worked on together in the past. He had been a customer of mine.

- I chose to introduce the job seeker to this particular person because he was in a field that interested the seeker and because I had a level of trust with both of them.

- I had no clue that the person I introduced him to would have a job available in his company. My expectation was that he would take time to hear what he had to say and would provide some advice and perhaps introduce him to a few other people he knew.

- I won't disclose details, but in this situation, a recent engineering school graduate who had been looking at mostly manufacturing jobs ended up with a job in the auto racing world. He had worked on cars with his dad for years, but he didn't see that as a gateway to getting a job in that field, due to the competition there. By the way, I don't know anything about racing, but I made the connection between "this guy worked on cars with his dad" and "that guy works in racing." It wasn't rocket science.

In summary, you should be networking to learn more about yourself and the jobs that might be a potential fit and to expand the reach of your search by getting more and more and more and more introductions.

Important note: PLEASE keep this chapter in mind not only when you are looking for a job, but also when someone tells you they are looking and want your help. Take the time to talk to them and to introduce them to others who might be able to help. It will have a bigger impact than simply looking at their resume!

CHAPTER 9

The Proven Path

I feel strongly that you will be well-served by employing the approaches laid out in this book. It is my sincere hope and prayer that from this point forward in your life, where you work and what you do will be in complete alignment with God's will for you. I am confident that His will for you is the best place for you to be!

I have intentionally not included anything in this book about interviewing or negotiating a job offer and the related salary and benefits. I've left that out for two reasons:

1. Like resume writing, there are tons of great resources available on both of those topics. I have been led to provide you with new insights on the process to get you to the right interview.

2. I believe deeply that the part of the process up to the interview is where most people go astray. Performing superbly in an interview and negotiating a killer deal

in a job you aren't created to have is a tragedy. It happens more often than it should. While I realize many people become scared that they will botch an interview for the perfect job and miss the opportunity of a lifetime, I'm convinced that is a rare occurrence.

Prior to giving some examples of how the Straight Path plays out in the real world, I'd like to review the major concepts.

- ✓ Ensure that you have appropriate views of work, per God's word. Work is incredibly important, but it is NOT what determines your worth to the Father.

- ✓ Assess your need for a new job. Before you embark on a job search, determine that you are not already "where you are supposed to be at this particular time."

- ✓ Establish a dedicated group of accountability partners to prayerfully guide you through the process.

- ✓ Take an inventory of your gifts, skills, and talents, and practice communicating them in different ways.

- ✓ Prepare your resume (I know if I left this out, I would have no credibility ☺)

- ✓ Network your butt off (that's a high-level business term).

- ✓ Land the job that aligns with God's will for you at this time.

And the real secret to success?

ALWAYS PRAY AND SEEK GODLY GUIDANCE.

CHAPTER 10

Tales From the Path

I truly hope that what I have shared in the previous chapters will provide new insights that will help you in finding the job to which God is calling you. Or, just as importantly, some of you may have realized you are already where you are supposed to be. That's worth celebrating as well!

I have decided to spend the final few pages sharing some examples from my life, about how this works in "the real world." I am sure that for some of you, the principles I have outlined seem abstract, and perhaps difficult to trust, in your particular situation. Many of the insights I have shared have come to me through my reading of God's word, conversations and observations from other Christians, and from the Holy Spirit in times of job turmoil for myself. I have learned from experience, paying attention to what was going on during job transitions for more than twenty-five years. The following "stories" are true and are from my own life and experience. I am 100% confident that thousands of others, maybe even you, have similar stories to tell.

> *Note: If you have a story to tell about how God guided you in a career transition, or away from a transition, we would love to hear about it. Please visit our website at www.straightenthepath.com and share your story.*

I Learned from the Best

The first real example I remember of noticing God at work in a career transition actually came as I observed my beautiful, amazing wife, Sharon, take a wild ride early in our marriage.

Out of college, Sharon went to work for the Internal Revenue Service (IRS) as a Revenue Agent. (I still laugh thinking about her grandfather joking with her about being a "revenuer.") She was highly successful there, was promoted rather quickly, and was working on large corporate cases at a young age.

Sharon and I were fairly new members at our local church, and we had been quickly recruited to work with the youth. You know how it goes…young couple with no kids…they don't have anything else to do…they would be great Youth Counselors!

We quickly got involved as Youth Counselors, supporting the Youth Director, and it became obvious almost immediately that Sharon had a gift for working with these knuckleheads…I mean young people. I enjoyed helping but always felt a bit like a fish out of water. Along the way, Sharon was asked to chair the new Youth Committee, to provide guidance to the young Youth Director, and keep things organized. Over time, the Youth Director left the role.

In his absence, Sharon and I were asked to step in and take a group of youth to a previously planned week-long mission work camp. We obliged, and that week changed things for both of us. Sharon had been having a few people in the church ask her if she would consider the Youth Director job at the church. She had always responded that she had a great job at the IRS (is that an oxymoron?) and it wasn't feasible. You see, Sharon is VERY practical. She doesn't do things like leaving a good government job with great benefits and great pay to work at the church for a third of the salary. That's just nonsense. Besides, she has an Accounting degree, not a Youth Worker degree. No one spends four years of college to get a degree and not use it!

As we spent our week at the camp with the kids, many of the camp counselors, other adult volunteers like us, and even some of the kids from the other churches complimented Sharon on the fine job she was doing. They continually told her what a great "Youth Director" she was, and they expressed how much they could tell the youth from our church loved her. She always responded with, "I'm not the Youth Director, I'm just a volunteer," but something had begun tugging at her heart.

Each night in camp, a day of hard physical work ended with a closing circle. All of the campers and staff would stand in a circle in an open field under the stars, and a camp counselor would pray, and have a devotion. One of the last nights of the week, they pulled a car into the field and turned on the car stereo super loud, playing a Steven Curtis Chapman song that neither of us had ever heard. The song is titled, "Waiting for Lightning."[6] One particular section of the lyrics hit Sharon hard. The Spirit was in on this...

> **Night falls and the curtain goes down**
> **No one's around, it's just you and the truth**
> **As you lie in wait for a feeling to take you by storm**
>
> **Somewhere in the depths of your heart**
> **Where it's empty and dark, there's a flicker of light**
> **And the spirit calls, but do you notice at all**
>
> **Are you waiting for lightning**
> **A sign that it's time for a change**
> **And you're listening for thunder**
> **While he quietly whispers your name**
>
> **But the sign and the word has already been given**
> **And now it's by faith, we must look and we must listen**
>
> **Instead of waiting for lightning**

Shortly after that night, we found ourselves considering something that would have seemed ridiculous only a month earlier. We knew it was the right thing and that it was God's will for Sharon to make this move. In the coming weeks, she discussed it with the church staff, asked for part-time status with the IRS, and became the Youth Director at our church. In the coming years, she would leave the IRS completely and focus full-time on youth ministry.

I know I am biased, but I have to tell you that I have never seen anyone be a more natural and complete fit for a job. While numbers in and of themselves are not relevant, over the next eight years, I watched the youth group at our church grow from single digit attendance to an average weekly attendance of sixty to seventy kids. I saw my beautiful wife minister to hurting youth and parents after a young teen in the group was killed in a car accident. I saw her shepherd young people as if it was all she was created to do. It was a beautiful thing.

Just as God called Sharon into youth ministry, over time, he called her out to watch over our two awesome children as they grew. As they became older, I saw her, yet again, go into a role as the Director of the Preschool at our church. Currently in that role, she has become one of the most powerful evangelists in our congregation, as she ministers to kids, teachers, and families as they struggle through the hard realities of life.

What's next for Sharon? I honestly have no clue. I am confident that there is plenty more for her to do and that she will continue to listen and go where God leads her.

Recently, a young woman who had been part of the youth group Sharon guided contacted her. She was in her mid-twenties and Sharon had not talked to or seen her in years. Sharon's mind was completely blown when she heard the request. "I am getting married, and I want you to marry us." You see, Sharon isn't an ordained minister. But it was clear to this young lady, as it is to me, that Sharon had ministered as powerfully during those years as a Youth Director, as anyone could have. The young couple was married this past year, by my wife and another Pastor. I don't think I've ever seen Sharon smile so big. God was smiling too. I'm totally sure of that.

Hard Headed!

Now that you have read the amazing story of my wife's obedience, I would like to share another scene from the career of the more hard-headed member of the family.

I was working in a subsidiary of a Fortune 100 company as the Director of Sales Operations. I had been on a great journey for about three and a half years with this group, and I had learned more than in any other segment of my career, to date.

Financially, the subsidiary was performing poorly, leadership was turning over rapidly, people were being laid off, and rumors of selling the firm were rampant. Once again, without consulting Sharon or my God, I forged out on my own. I contacted a consulting firm, and before long, I was interviewing for a job as a partner in the firm. Sharon was uncomfortable with it, because she knew almost nothing about it, and the company was in Arkansas. Nothing personal against Arkansas, by the way, except that we lived in North Carolina, always had, and in Sharon's mind, always will. We had a baby boy at this point and had started to notice some developmental issues, so we were spending a lot of time with doctors and tests.

As I continued the discussions, I assured Sharon that we would not have to move, though I would be travelling quite a bit. I had convinced the firm that I could be effective from North Carolina, and I was open to as much travel as necessary, whether it be to Arkansas to learn or to clients' locations across the United States. Not for a minute did I pause to pray and ask for guidance. You see, this was honestly my "dream job." Just like in the scenario I described in Chapter 1, my ego kicked in and I lost all ability to be rational. I talked to friends about it and said that I "felt" that God created this job for me.

Sharon and I argued quite a bit about this one, but I forged ahead. The company flew me to California to sit in on a live client engagement, to see if I was a fit. That went great. They called me and scheduled for me to come to the headquarters to have final discussions. I was elated, and Sharon was furious. All I could see was my dream job. All she could see was her taking care of a little boy on her own, while dad was flying around the country.

About a week before I was to fly out for the final interview, I got a call from the founder of the firm. "John," he said, "we met as a management team yesterday, and we have decided for this to work out, you are going to have to move to Little Rock." Apparently, they had recently let several consultants go that weren't working out. The common theme was that all of them were working remotely, and it had been too difficult to assimilate to the firm from a distance. They offered for me to bring Sharon out to Little Rock with me and have her look around if we wanted to still consider it. Yeah, that's gonna happen!

I went home, with my tail between my legs, prepared to just forget it. I told Sharon what they said and that I knew that it wasn't meant to be. Her response: "Book the flight. We have to go." What? Had she lost her mind? She had made it perfectly clear that she wanted no part of moving...ever! She went on to explain that we had to be absolutely sure. And that we needed to not leave the door cracked open, but to find out what was "supposed to happen here." She blew me away that day (again!) with her commitment to me and to figuring out God's will. We began to pray together about it, like we should have for the previous month, and asked God to show us his will.

On the day of the flight, we arrived at the airport plenty early and waited at the gate for our flight to Arkansas. Shortly before departure time, the sign at the gate changed to "Flight Cancelled." What!? No way!! But wait, we asked for God to make his will clear. Though my heart hurt at the thought of this not working out, I had a sense of peace for the first time about the whole situation.

I said to Sharon, with a genuine smile on my face, "Well, I guess that about does it. Let's head home." She looked at me calmly and said, "Nope. We have to be sure. Let's go see if we can catch another flight." *Are you insane?* (I thought this, but used wisdom and did not say it!). She grabbed my hand and pulled me off toward the service desk, where we found that there was another flight, but we literally had to run to catch it. And we did.

On the plane, we both had a sense of peace. Not that we knew what was going to happen, but a peace that comes with realizing that you are going after God's will and that you know things will turn out right, no matter what "right" may be.

When we arrived in Little Rock, Sharon jumped in the car with a realtor, and I went to the firm's office to do a requested presentation. They wanted to see how I handled myself in a setting similar to the one I would be in with their high profile clients. I had picked a topic that I had presented a dozen times, and my confidence was strong. It is important to note here that I am one of those people who tests better than what they really know. When the pressure is the highest, I am normally at my best. To sum up what happened next, I will simply say it was awful. I stammered, stuttered, and didn't even make sense to myself. I handled questions poorly, and it was a disaster. The feeling in the room was awkward, because we all knew that this was a mistake.

No one said much, but they drove me back to the hotel where I was to meet Sharon and prepare to go out to dinner with the team. I walked in the door, and Sharon asked, "How did it go?" I burst into tears, fell on the bed and said "It was horrible. This is not where we are supposed to be." She said, "Good, because I hate it here!" We both laughed and cried and got ready for dinner. They were gracious and treated us well during dinner, though we all worked hard to not talk about the job, knowing how badly things had gone.

I got a call the next day from the founder. "This just doesn't seem to be a fit right now." I agreed and thanked him for investing so much time into the process.

Note: The one thing I didn't mention about this whole scenario is that the guys in this firm were strong Christian people. They were open about their faith and the founder had even written a book about "finding the right career." The fact that it was a Christian business clouded my thinking along the way, I believe. I somehow bought into the fact that because it was "Christian," it had to be right for me. Clearly not so. I think they were praying, too!

The River Revisited

If you recall the scenes from Chapter 1, when I basically talked myself out of a job, you may have wondered what happened next.

After gaining the insight that I had ignored God in the process, I reached out to him like never before and prayed for guidance and a second chance. I swallowed my pride (that was quite a mouthful) and called a former boss in the big company I was in and told him what had happened and asked for help. Within a couple of weeks, I had a new role that was a perfect fit for me, in a new subsidiary that was just being formed.

Not only was it a good opportunity, but it provided what I had wanted all along. It gave me the tremendous opportunity for professional growth and the ability to make a difference in a smaller office, while also providing the stability of being owned by the larger firm. It is likely that I would have been contacted about that role within a week or so, even if I hadn't taken matters into my own hands and almost lost my job. I tried to outrun God. God's timing is MUCH better than mine.

It's "Simple"

This final example from my career is both the most powerful and the most recent example of how God has played a vital role in my career transitions. You see, this time, I took the right approach from the beginning.

I was in an amazing job as the Southeast Director for a technology firm headquartered in the Northeast. I had been there for about four years and had learned a great deal about business, sales, and leadership, in a highly competitive marketplace. Our Southeast team had grown every year I was there, including during the difficult economy of 2007 – 2009. By 2010, our team made up half of the company's revenue and profits, while having less than a fourth of the company's resources. I was making significantly more money than I had in any other job. But there was trouble in paradise.

It had become clear that the company was having some financial challenges, and the word on the street was that the company was for sale. Our team's numbers were solid, so I didn't think a sale would have much of an impact on me or the Southeast team.

While I was not "looking for a job," I had been discussing a potential role with the owners of a local firm that seemed like it had some promise for me. I had been introduced to them by one of their sisters-in-law, with whom I had worked in my current job, but never actually met face to face (there's that networking thing again). I met with the managing partners numerous times over a period of several months, and we seemed to be in excellent alignment, both personally and professionally. It was a small firm (eight people at the time), and they had never had anyone in a dedicated business development role. The partners had looked for and secured business, and then worked on the delivery side of things until the projects started wrapping up and then went after the next project.

They said they weren't sure they were ready for a role like mine, but knew company growth would require it at some point. Talks continued for several months. During this time, for the first time ever, I truly committed the entire process to the Lord from the beginning. I prayed about it. I fasted. I committed to not worrying about it and honestly was at peace the entire time. If it worked out I wanted it to be God's will. If it didn't, I wanted that to be in alignment with his plan for me as well.

I had a meeting scheduled with the owners of the potential firm for a Tuesday in July, to discuss what a compensation package might look like, and to discuss when a transition would make sense if we reached an agreement. They were not in any hurry to take on my salary, and I had a steady flow of commissions coming in from my current job and didn't want to walk away from that. Both sides were committed to not rushing, and we had even discussed that it might be best to wait until the first of the year, or at least October, to make a transition, if we agreed to move forward at all.

I had begun to share the scenario with a few close friends, and they held me accountable to continually being prayerful about it. Sharon and I were on the same page and were at peace with whatever happened, because we were committed to following the Holy Spirit's promptings, and not moving without that.

The Sunday before the scheduled meeting on Tuesday with the prospective company, Sharon and I were leading a lesson on prayer in our Sunday School class. We had been studying the topic of prayer for several weeks and had begun the practice of having a volunteer sit in a chair in the middle of the room at the end of each class and share a prayer concern. The rest of the class would then lay hands on the person and pray.

On this particular Sunday, no one volunteered. Not sure what to do, I said I would do it and shared with the class that while I had an incredible job that most people would say I'd be nuts to leave, another opportunity was being presented. I explained that Sharon and I were peaceful about it, and we were concerned only that we do God's will and asked that they pray for wisdom for us, regarding the meeting that was two days away.

Everyone prayed, but the thing that stood out most was Sharon's prayer. She prayed aloud, with her hands on me, "God, make it simple." We had both worked hard to not worry or strive over the decision, and we had enjoyed that sense of peace, in contrast with the turmoil that accompanied many of my earlier job transitions.

The next day, on Monday morning, I was meeting with an employee who worked for me when my phone rang around 10:00 a.m. It was my boss, one of the owners of the company. "Can you talk?" he asked. I said, "Not right now, I have someone in my office." He asked me to call him as soon as I could.

I wrapped up my meeting quickly and called him back. He answered the phone and in plain and simple words he said, "We've sold the company, I have to let you go."

A little shocked, but not freaking out, I asked about details. My boss told me I needed to be out of the office by noon (that was less than two hours away) and that I would be paid through the end of the week.

That was it. Four years of hard work, brought to an abrupt end in 30 seconds.

I walked out the door, somewhat in a daze. I got to my car, and just before I dialed Sharon's number, I remembered her prayer. "Make it simple." I guess it doesn't get much simpler than that.

After calling Sharon, who was ridiculously calm and supportive, I reminded her of the prayer. We chuckled, and I said, "I think I need to call the other company."

When I reached out and explained my situation, the answer I heard from the other end of the phone was simply, "I guess we better hurry up."

I had a scheduled meeting on Tuesday, and my first day on the job was on Thursday. I could not see the path ahead, but God could not only see it, but he also straightened it.

CHAPTER 11

Final Thoughts

My deepest prayer is that you have gained some useful insight through the words in this book. I truly feel blessed and honored to have been given the opportunity to write it.

There are two important final points that I want to leave with you.

First, I want to ensure that you understand that what I am suggesting is not an easy "recipe" for getting a great job. While some of the examples I shared seem straightforward as I've told them, I assure you that things rarely seemed clear and organized at the time. Searching for and discerning God's will can be quite taxing and confusing. However, we should be greatly encouraged by the words from James 1:2-6:

> Consider it pure joy, my brothers and sisters, whenever you face trials of many kinds, because you know that the testing of your faith

> produces perseverance. Let perseverance finish its work so that you may be mature and complete, not lacking anything. If any of you lacks wisdom, you should ask God, who gives generously to all without finding fault, and it will be given to you. But when you ask, you must believe and not doubt, because the one who doubts is like a wave of the sea, blown and tossed by the wind.

When you place your confidence in the Creator of the Universe, He will show you the way.

We can't treat God like a vending machine and say "what do you want me to do," push a button, and expect an answer to fall out of the sky. We can't treat God as if he is the dessert at the end of a meal in a Chinese restaurant and expect his answer to be in a fortune cookie. Though I'm confident God could handle it either way, or in a multitude of other ways if he chose to, we would miss out on the incredible growth from the journey.

Finally, my premise for all you have read is simply this:

God cares deeply about your work and the job you have.

In 1 Corinthians 12: 15-18 the apostle Paul writes:

> Now if the foot should say, "Because I am not a hand, I do not belong to the body," it would not for that reason stop being part of the body. And if the ear should say, "Because I am not an eye, I do not belong to the body," it would not for that reason stop being part of the body. If the whole body were an eye, where would the sense of hearing be? If the whole body were an ear, where would the sense of smell be? **But in fact God has placed the parts in the body, every one of them, just as he wanted them to be** (emphasis mine).

Did you read that last part? My prayer is that you will diligently seek God's will and spend the rest of your life allowing him to place you where he wants you to be. Because, you see, he loves you and wants what is best for you.

In Jeremiah 29:11 we are encouraged with these words.

> For I know the plans I have for you," declares the Lord, "plans to prosper you and not to harm you, plans to give you hope and a future.

Don't try to figure out the plans without him. His plans will prosper you and give you hope and a future!

I thought it was amazing that on the day that I am writing the last chapter of this book, the daily devotion that I read contains this remarkable quote from Derek Prince in *Declaring God's Word:*

> ...the choice of where and what we are to be in the body is not ours, but God's. God has arranged the members of His body and assigned their functions. It is not for us to decide; rather, God decides and reveals His decisions to us.[7]

That sums it up completely. In searching for a job, most of us could stand to do a lot less planning and researching, and a lot more praying and listening. Make sure you are listening to the one who created the world!

I am convinced that each of us has a specific place we are meant to be, at any point in time, in God's Kingdom. I am equally convinced that His Kingdom does not function as effectively as it is intended to, unless each of us is effectively functioning in the role to which He is calling us, whether it be a banker, an engineer, a store clerk, a doctor, a pastor, a full-time mom or dad, or a plasma physicist.

Thy Will Be Done, On Earth, as it is in Heaven!

MESSAGE FROM THE AUTHOR

Thank you for reading my book! I pray you find it helpful as you search for your dream job. Allow God to do the recruiting to place you exactly where he wants you to be—that is the true "straight path" to a successful job search.

If you could take just a moment to go to Amazon.com and leave a review for my book, I would appreciate it so much. Thank you!

I want to extend a personal invitation to you to visit the website www.straightenthepath.com to learn more and to share your stories. Check out my blog, and learn about upcoming speaking engagements and workshops. You will also find useful links for lots of good, *free* job search information!

All the best in your job search, and may God ever be exalted for his mercy and love. Amen.

ABOUT THE AUTHOR

Growing up in a small North Carolina town, John Freeze embraced the American dream, earning a B.S. degree in Electrical Engineering. Later, he attended college at night, while working full-time, to obtain a Master's Degree in Business Administration with a concentration in Organizational Behavior. His life experiences in small-town America coupled with his education, work experience, and training uniquely qualify him to do the work he considers his ministry – helping others in using God's time-tested principles to ensure there is alignment between their earthly and spiritual lives, specifically as it relates to job searches.

With 25+ years of work experience ranging from working in a Fortune 100 company to being the ninth employee of a consulting firm that would later be recognized as an Inc. 5000 winner, John has held management and staff roles in IT, sales, marketing, accounting, operations, engineering, and human resources. He has interviewed literally hundreds of people for various jobs from entry-level to Vice Presidents, and he has had an active role in staffing four different organizations. John has the perspective to guide others along their path to a dream job. He truly understands today's challenging job market, and he knows what it takes to help you find the right career path for you.

John still resides in North Carolina, with his amazing wife of 26 years, Sharon. They have two incredible kids, Ian (19) and Jasey (15), whom they adopted from Paraguay and Guatemala. The family is active in their local church, where John and Sharon have served in various leadership roles for over 20 years.

John is available for speaking engagements and can be contacted via his website at www.straightenthepath.com. He is currently working on additional books on networking and other job-search-related topics. Look for his next book, *Crowds Along the Path: Networking is Not a Four-Letter Word*, and visit the website for updates and other information.

END NOTES

[1] Doug Spada and Dave Scott, *Monday Morning Atheist*, (Alpharetta, GA: WorkLife Press, 2012).

[2] Tom Rath, *StrengthsFinder 2.0*, (New York: Gallup Press, 2007).

[3] Anna B. Warner (lyrics) and William B. Bradbury (music), *"Jesus Loves Me,"* 1862. Song and lyrics are in the public domain. http://library.timelesstruths.org/music/Jesus_Loves_Me/ (October 24, 2014).

[4] Max Lucado, *Facing Your Giants* (Nashville, TN: Thomas Nelson, 2006), 170.

[5] Dick Wolfe, "ADP National Employment Report Shows 181,000 Jobs Added in June," *ADP Research Institute*, www.adpemploymentreport.com/2014/June/NER/NER-June-2014.aspx (September 15, 2014).

[6] Steven Curtis Chapman and Tony Elenburg, "Waiting for Lightning," © 1989 Birdwing Music (ASCAP) Sparrow Song (BMI) Greg Nelson Music (BMI) Universal Music – Brentwood Benson Songs (BMI) (adm. at CapitolCMGPublishing.com). All rights reserved. Used by permission.

[7] Derek Prince, *Declaring God's Word: A 365-Day Devotional*, (Charlotte, NC: Whitaker House, 2008), 240.

www.ingramcontent.com/pod-product-compliance
Lightning Source LLC
Chambersburg PA
CBHW051721170526
45167CB00002B/755